THE CARING

GOD

BIBLICAL MODELS OF DISCIPLESHIP

DAVID M. SCHOLER

Judson Press® Valley Forge

THE CARING GOD

Library of Congress Cataloging-in-Publication Data
Scholer, David M.
    The caring God.
    Bibliography: p.
    1. Caring—Biblical teaching.   2. Caring—Religious aspects—Christianity.
3. Providence and government of God—Biblical teaching.   I. Title.
BS680.C37S36 1989   241'.4   88-32872
ISBN 0-8170-1152-8

To

Milton and Bernice Scholer,

my parents,
two of my greatest
teachers and examples
of our caring God

Preface

It was an honor and privilege to give the three plenary lectures at the Grow By Caring National Gathering at the American Baptist Assembly, Green Lake, Wis., April 14–18, 1986. This book presents a slightly revised form of those lectures. It is my hope that this volume will be of help and encouragement to many persons in various contexts.

I want to thank the many persons who played a role in bringing this book to completion, especially the Grow By Caring Committee (Ken Blazier and Ruthie Popjoy in particular), who invited me to give the lectures; the denominational leaders at the American Baptist Assembly, who so warmly affirmed these presentations; Patricia Slowik, who typed the manuscript; William Cober, who coordinated the process leading to publication; and the editors at Judson Press, who prepared the manuscript for publication.

David M. Scholer
November 4, 1988

Contents

Introduction

How does an individual or a church learn to care? I suggest that the answer is integrity, being genuine in our caring. We must *earn* the right to care.

It is my focus and intent in these three chapters to provide selective and basic biblical/theological perspectives and reflections on caring and the importance of caring as the fundamental means and reality needed for all dimensions of growth in the church. It is not my intent here to discuss the definitions and issues of growth. We all share, I suspect, deep concern over the patent abuses in the church today related to the church growth concept. Our common sense of integrity has made us recoil from false emphases on numerical growth. We know that size never is a criterion of the genuine work of God. Rather, we understand that genuine motivation and faithfulness to the gospel and integrity are the true criteria. Yet growth can and should take place in the church both numerically and qualitatively. Ignoring either is shallow and evasive.

I have found helpful the four aspects of growth that have been identified by a number of writers, including the late Orlando E. Costas, former dean of Andover Newton Theological School, and Emmett V. Johnson, director of evangelism for the American Baptist Churches in the U.S.A.

Numerical growth is the first of those four. Here I will quote my favorite New Testament text with respect to the numerical growth of the church. It comes from one of John's visions in Revelation:

> After this I looked, and behold, a great multitude which no one could number, from every nation, from all tribes and peoples and tongues, standing before the throne and before the Lamb, clothed in white robes, with palm branches in their hands, and crying out with a loud voice, "Salvation belongs to our God who sits upon the throne, and to the Lamb!" (Revelation 7:9–10).

The second aspect of growth is **organic growth** or growing together—the emphasis upon the unity and community in the Body of Christ.

Third, **conceptual growth** or growing up: the sense of discipleship, responsibility, and maturity in the faith.

Fourth, **incarnational growth** or growing out—the ministry of love and justice to the church and the world.

It is my intent to cause us to think deeply and maybe even be a little disturbed as we reflect on caring and the importance of caring.

I understand caring to be an expression of concern for and responsible engagement with another, grounded in genuine respect and love, the goal of which is the affirmation and nurture of the other, with accountability that sees the other

Introduction

to be fully and with integrity what God intends that one to be.

Caring in its ultimate sense is an activity of God and those created in God's image directed toward individuals, churches, and the church and the world both in its social and ecological dimensions.

Chapter 1

The Caring God:

Reflections on God's Care in the Old Testament

It is the very character of God to be caring. Our understanding of God as Creator of the earth, the universe, and persons in God's image, and our understanding of God as Redeemer and Savior are fundamental expressions of God's caring.

One story that has moved me greatly was told to me sometime ago about Nels Ferré. The story is true.

Nels Ferré was a visiting faculty member at Vanderbilt Divinity School. A doctoral student in one of his classes came out of a very strict fundamentalist background. One thing the student knew was that Nels Ferré probably wasn't safe or trustworthy. Yet that student had this professor again and again in his doctoral studies, and Nels Ferré became the person with whom he related most often. In the course of time this student, who was married and had a very small child, came to a day of tragedy. The young child of this student and his wife inexplicably became very ill. Suddenly, a few days later, in the middle of the night, the little child died. The student and his wife were in great distress and didn't know what to do. The only person they could think of calling was Nels Ferré. In the middle of the night, the student called his professor. Nels Ferré came to that student apartment where this husband and wife were weeping. He sat down with them, put his arms around them, and remained for three or four hours without uttering a word. Then he got up to go. As he hugged the husband and wife, he said, "God is weeping, too."

It is too easy and potentially damaging to romanticize an understanding of God as caring. There are at least two basic obstacles that must be recognized and faced if we are to have integrity in our understanding of God as caring.

The first to be confronted is the classic problem of evil. Perhaps no statement, as it affects understanding God as caring, is as piercing and powerful as that of Elie Wiesel in his 1958 book *Night* about the virtually indescribable agonies and horrors of the Holocaust. After describing the background of arriving at the death camp and experiencing the first night, Wiesel writes:

> Never shall I forget that night, the first night in the camp, which has turned my life into one long night, seven times cursed and seven times sealed . . . . Never shall I forget those flames which consumed my faith forever. Never shall I forget that nocturnal silence which deprived me, for all eternity, of the desire to live. Never shall I forget those moments which murdered my God and my soul and turned my dreams to dust.[1]

This is not the place to attempt to solve the problem. In fact, it cannot be solved. Rather, we affirm that God is a God of love and care known and claimed in the midst of suffering and evil. As Christians we believe that God in Christ has demonstrated victory over evil. Nevertheless, as persons with integrity and sensitivity toward others, we can never speak glibly, facilely, or without humility of the care of God.

The second matter to be addressed is the common Christian perception of God as angry and vindictive. How could such a God care? Perhaps some of you have read the story told by Shirley Guthrie, Jr., in his book *Christian Doctrine.*

Once upon a time a boy went to a revival meeting. He had grown up in a Christian home and in the church, but he heard something that night he had never heard before. The preacher held up a very dirty water glass.

"See this glass? That's you. Filthy, stained with sin, inside and outside."

He picked up a hammer.

"This hammer is the righteousness of God. It is the instrument of his wrath against sinful men. His justice can be satisfied only by punishing and destroying sinners whose lives are filled with vileness and corruption."

He put the glass on the pulpit and slowly, deliberately drew back the hammer clenched in his fist, took deadly aim, and with all his might let the blow fall.

But a miracle happened! At the last moment the preacher covered the glass with a pan. The hammer struck the pan with a crash that echoed through the hushed church. He held up the untouched glass with one hand and the mangled pan with the other and made his point.

"Jesus Christ died for your sins. He took the punishment which ought to have fallen on you. He satified the righteousness of God that you might go free if you believe in him."

When he went to bed that night, the boy could not sleep. Meditating on what he had seen and heard, he decided that he was terribly afraid of God. How could he love such a God? He could love Jesus, who had sacrificed himself for him. But how could he love a God who wanted to "get" everyone and was only kept from doing it because Jesus got in the way? The thought crossed the boy's mind that he could only hate such a hammer-swinging God who had to be bought off at such a terrible price. But he quickly dismissed the thought. That very God might read his mind and punish him.[2]

Without denying the integrity of deep theological issues related to the understanding of the necessity and nature of the atonement, I think it should be clear that the whole Bible, holistically understood, presents God as one who loves, initiates love, forgives, initiates forgiveness, and exhibits longsuffering and patience. The view of God as so angry and vindictive, which has psychologically and theologically confused so many persons in the church, is tragic and wrong. Let's return to the valid issue of God's judgment and caring.

From the vast storehouse of the Hebrew Scriptures that we call the Old Testament, I want to draw our attention now to three facets of the caring God: 1) God's steadfast love for Israel; 2) God's concern for the poor, the widow, the orphan, and the alien; and 3) God's love for and attention to nations outside of Israel.

First, we'll look at God's steadfast love for Israel as a facet of the caring God. In virtually every strand of its traditions and genres of literature, the Old Testament witnesses powerfully to the affirmation of God's care and steadfast love for Israel. This often is expressed in the face of Israel's disobedience and neglect and often in conjunction with Israel's praise of God. Listen to this marvelous and very selective litany from the range of Scripture that evidences Israel's sense of knowing a caring God.

From the Pentateuch, Exodus chapter 34 recounts the renewal of the Covenant when Moses ascends Mount Sinai and the Lord

> . . . passed before him, and proclaimed, "The LORD, the LORD, a God merciful and gracious, slow to anger, and abounding in steadfast love and faithfulness, keeping steadfast love for thousands, forgiving iniquity and transgression and sin . . . " (Exodus 34:6-7).

Almost identical language is repeated when Moses, in Numbers chapter 14, pleads for Israel when they are afraid to enter the land and are grumbling against God:

> "And now, I pray thee, let the power of the LORD be great as thou hast promised, saying, 'The LORD is slow to anger, and abounding in steadfast love, forgiving iniquity and transgression . . . .' Pardon the iniquity of this people, I pray thee, according to the greatness of thy steadfast love, and according as thou hast forgiven this people, from Egypt even until now" (Numbers 14:17-19).

The prophets, too, sound this same theme of God's care for Israel.

> "For the mountains may depart
>   and the hills be removed,
> but my steadfast love shall not
>   depart from you,
> and my covenant of peace shall
>   not be removed,
> says the LORD, who has
>   compassion on you"
>   (Isaiah 54:10).

and

"Incline your ear, and come to me;
hear, that your soul may live;
and I will make with you an
everlasting covenant,
my steadfast, sure love for David"
(Isaiah 55:3).

In Joel it is declared:

"Return to the LORD, your God,
for [God] is gracious and merciful,
slow to anger, and abounding in
steadfast love,
and repents of evil"
(Joel 2:13).

Who can forget the power of Hosea's charge from God:

"Go again, love a woman who is beloved of a paramour and
is an adulteress; even as the LORD loves the people of Israel,
though they turn to other gods and love cakes of raisins"
(Hosea 3:1).

In Nehemiah is the record of Israel's return from captivity.
There is recorded there that great prayer of Israel (ascribed
in some but not all manuscripts to Ezra), part of which
confesses after a recitation of Israel's disobedience and dis-
belief:

"But thou art a God ready to forgive, gracious and merciful,
slow to anger and abounding in steadfast love, and thou didst
not forsake them" (Nehemiah 9:17).

Of course, the Psalms are replete with this confession of
God's care. The praise of Psalm 86:

> But thou, O Lord, art a God
> merciful and gracious,
> slow to anger and abounding in
> steadfast love and faithfulness
> (Psalm 86:15).

That is repeated virtually verbatim in Psalms 103 and 145 (103:8; 145:8). Psalms 103, 106, and 107 are especially rich in repeated litanies and strong affirmations of God's care, even in the face of Israel's sin, rebellion, and unfaithfulness:

> Bless the LORD, O my soul,
> and forget not all [the] benefits,
> who forgives all your iniquity,
> who heals all your diseases . . . ,
> who crowns you with steadfast
> love and mercy . . . .
> The LORD works vindication
> and justice for all who are
> oppressed
> (Psalm 103:2-4, 6).

> O give thanks to the LORD, for
> [the LORD] is good;
> for [the LORD's] steadfast love endures for
> ever!
> (Psalm 107:1).

In the face of this powerful witness of the Hebrew Scriptures to God's steadfast love and care for Israel, a few observations need to be made, even if difficult. First, it is not surprising to me that Frederick Holmgren entitled his book about a Christian approach to Judaism *The God Who Cares.*[3] Much of the Christian tradition has unfairly and inaccurately portrayed God in the ancient Jewish view as being a legalist who related to Israel in legalistic terms. The Christian view of Judaism, almost always a caricature, even has led to various forms of anti-Semitism in Christian theological scholarship, as has been demonstrated by the German theologian Charlotte Klein.[4] Although the Law was central to Judaism and obedience to the Law was the only appropriate response to God's Covenant, it must not be forgotten that the basis of God's relationship to Israel and Israel's inclusion in the Covenant always was God's gracious mercy, steadfast love, and initiative of forgiveness.[5]

Second, honest thought and integrity mean that we must deal with the so-called "other side" of some of these great and glorious passages about God's care. Some of these affirmations include, in immediate conjunction and direct contrast, a statement of God's judgment and condemnation of the wicked who do not repent. The resolution of such theological issues, hardly limited to the Old Testament, has troubled the church for a long time. However, we constantly must reflect on such searching questions. I have two observations for now.

The first observation is psychological. I have discovered, often to my horror and shame, that I sometimes have not cared what happened to certain persons. I did not feel anger or condemnation for certain persons precisely because I cared so little or, in fact, not at all. My observation out of this experience is that judgment is, in its own peculiar way, a function of caring.

My second observation is a theological one borrowed from American Baptist theologian Mark Heim. In his 1985 book *Is Christ the Only Way?*, Heim grapples with many deep questions about the Christian claim of salvation in Christ, including this broad scriptural issue of God's judgment. He wrote:

> The key to this popular image . . . assumes that all people are meted out their faith or condemned against their wills . . . . According to this warped interpretation, people have been rounded up and imprisoned, and will pay an eternal price . . . . At this crucial point the popular image could hardly be further off the mark. The point of judgment is not some arbitrary cutoff. Judgment is inseparable from the notion of . . . [God's] . . . new reality. Those who do not participate in it are not just in neutral. They continue to be transformed in other ways. It is not that God will not give people a second chance, or a third or a fourth. The simple fact is that we can reach a point when a thousand chances would not make a difference. If they would, they would be given.[6]

Second, I want to look briefly at God's concern for the poor, the widow, the orphan, and the alien in the land of Israel as another facet of the caring God.

This concern of God and evidence of God's care also is found powerfully in the different genres of the Old Testament. Psalm 9:16 (NIV) declares that "The Lord is known by his justice. . . ." All four groups of God's special concern in justice are mentioned when

> . . . the word of the Lord came again to Zechariah: "This is what the Lord Almighty says: 'Administer true justice; show mercy and compassion to one another. Do not oppress the widow or the fatherless, the alien or the poor' " (Zechariah 7:8-10, NIV).

This love and concern of God for those who are helpless or threatened in the face of those who had the power and controlled society, even when those who had the power and controlled society were among God's own people, is a powerful statement and insight into the nature and commitment of God's care. We read earlier Psalm 103:6, which stated that "The LORD works vindication and justice for all who are oppressed." This care for the alien, the widow, the orphan, and the poor also is expressed in the Law and in the Psalms as well as elsewhere in the Prophets.[7] (Biblical concern for the poor, oppressed, and neglected persons is pursued at length in the second chapter.)

The third facet of God's care is God's love for and attention to nations outside of Israel, which especially is illustrated so powerfully in the story of Jonah. Unfortunately, controversies over the book of Jonah often have obscured the powerful message of this prophetic work. Too often disputes over the historicity of Jonah and/or the believability of Jonah's experience with the great fish have so dominated concern that the actual intent of this book in the canon of Scripture is overlooked. Even homileticians and preachers have clouded matters at times by moralizing on Jonah's avoidance of the clear call of God on his life.

It is striking, even stunning, that Jonah's struggle and failure grew directly out of his clear and unambiguous understanding of the first facet of God's care to which we gave attention. When Jonah finally went to alien and wicked Nineveh, the capital of Assyria, an enemy of Israel, and they repented, God also repented and withdrew judgment against Nineveh. But Jonah did not repent. Jonah was angry. He did not moralize as to why he went to Tarshish to avoid the call of God. No, Jonah had a fundamental theological reason for his initial flight away from Nineveh and for his anger over Nineveh's repentance—and God's repentance. Jonah said to God:

"...for I knew that thou art a gracious God and merciful, slow to anger, and abounding in steadfast love, and repentest of evil" (Jonah 4:2).

These are the same words that we heard in the Law, the Prophets, the historical work of Nehemiah and the Psalms. Jonah never really changes. He knows God to be caring. He cannot accept the fact that God's care extends beyond the limits Jonah has set for his own vision. God's care is exhibited in God's love for and attention to Nineveh, a place and a symbol to demonstrate God's universal care and steadfast love.

In many ways, we might observe that Jonah is not unlike the older brother, at whom we will look in the second chapter, who cannot accept the love and forgiveness of his father toward his younger, prodigal brother.

In conclusion, we have seen the caring God in the Old Testament in three major facets of care that can be instructive for us as the people of God, both for ourselves and for our mission in the world. God's care is displayed in steadfast love that is gracious, merciful, slow to anger, and forgiving. God's care is displayed in God's commitment to justice as evidenced in God's concern for the widow, the orphan, the alien, and the poor. God's care is displayed in God's attention to Nineveh, a powerful symbol of God's universal concern that so often shatters our boundaries based on self-centered understanding of God's love (that in the final analysis is a misunderstanding).

May these three facets of God's care and caring be for us models and components of our own commitment to care in the church and its mission in the world today.

Chapter 2

The Caring Christ:

Jesus' Care for Marginalized People in the Gospel of Luke

I have been impressed, maybe you have too, with Jaroslav Pelikan's major 1985 book that has attracted so much attention: *Jesus Through the Centuries: His Place in the History of Culture.* [1] It has been fascinating and broadening for me to read this book, both as a New Testament scholar and as a Christian thinker whose faith and culture have been shaped by so many of the events and images that Pelikan artfully describes.

As you may know, his book presents eighteen images portraying Jesus' place in the history of culture, especially Western culture. Pelikan names each of these eighteen, and as I observed to the planning team for this event, not one of the images is called "Caregiver." The images that Pelikan has are Rabbi, Turning Point of History, Light of the Gentiles, King of kings, Cosmic Christ, Son of Man, True Image, Christ Crucified, the Monk Who Rules the World, Bridegroom of the Soul, Divine and Human Model, Universal Man, Mirror of the Eternal, Prince of Peace, Teacher of

Common Sense, Poet of the Spirit and Man Who Belongs to the World. That's only seventeen. There is one that comes very close to Caregiver; so close that it's virtually the same. It's the image of Christ as Liberator. This is Pelikan's description of what he means by that image:

> Throughout the nineteenth and twentieth centuries, from Tolstoy to Mahatma Gandhi to Martin Luther King, Jr., the use of Jesus' prophetic opposition to the economic and social injustice of his time [is seen] as the dynamic for revolutionary change in the ordering of human relations, public as well as private.[2]

As I indicated earlier in my definition of caring, the goal of caring is the affirmation and nurture that frees or liberates one to be fully and with integrity what God intends that one be.

I believe that the most complete and most powerful presentation of Jesus as a liberating or caregiving Christ in the New Testament is found in the Gospel of Luke and in Luke's strong story and proclamation of Jesus' care for persons who were considered marginal in his time and who were demeaned, deprived, and oppressed in his own time and place. The Lukan presentation of Jesus' care for others can be instructive for us as people of God, both for ourselves and for our mission in the world.

Some attention ought to be given to the importance, value, and need of looking at each Gospel in the New Testament canon on its own. Spiro Agnew once said "If you've seen one slum, you've seen them all." Some years later, as I was teaching the Synoptic Gospels, it occurred to me one day to take off on that phrase: "If you've read one Gospel, you have not read them all!" One of the goals of my New

Testament teaching is to help persons understand that part of the glory of the canon is that there are four Gospels, not one. The inheritance of almost every one of us is a "homogenized" life of Jesus. We learn the life of Jesus that has been woven together from the Four Gospels, and often from other places, too, and we understand this life of Jesus and hardly ever can sort out what came from Matthew, what came from Mark, what came from Luke, and what came from John. I think one of the importances of understanding the New Testament canon as we have it, if we are people of the Book, is to recognize that there are four different Gospels in the canon and that one of our obligations as good students of the Bible is to be able to articulate and to claim the presentation of each Gospel writer.

One day, when I was teaching in another seminary, I had lectured on the importance of recognizing especially each Synoptic Gospel and not trying to collapse them into one. After class, a student approached me in the hallway. I could tell by the fire in his eyes that he was upset. He walked right up to me until he practically knocked me over, and he shook his finger right in my face and said, "God would never give us more than one Gospel." Now you realize where he was coming from. I think that for many of us we know it still is true that it's difficult in our churches to talk about the distinctive perspectives of a particular Gospel.

This particular mode of scholarship often is called redaction criticism, a very useful methodological development in New Testament studies. It is the recognition of the intentions and perspectives of particular Gospel writers that are reflected in what they select to include in their Gospels, how they arrange the material, and how they shape it and reshape it for the intentionality of what they wish to say. This often is seen best in what is unique in a particular Gospel; at least such distinctive or unique elements in a Gospel help us to identify clearly the concerns of the Gospel writer and his presentation of the traditions of Jesus. Further, it is understood that the motivation of the writer for his selection, arrangement, and reshaping of Jesus' material comes as much from the context to which he is speaking as it does from the tradition that he accepts and inherits to pass on to the readers of his Gospel.

The Gospel of Luke, without question my favorite Gospel, is the one that is most relevant to the presentation of Jesus as a caring person. This Gospel has two fundamental themes that characterize its presentation of Jesus and account for its selection, arrangement, and reshaping of the traditions about the life and teachings of Jesus.

The first of those two fundamental themes is radical discipleship and its consequent implications concerning wealth and material possessions. Clearly related to that first theme is the second: concern for marginalized persons—persons who were demeaned, deprived of care, and oppressed in Jesus' own time.

It is generally thought by scholars today that the Gospel of Luke most likely was addressed to a church or group of churches that was/were struggling with many issues, but particularly with the demand of radical discipleship that affected one's view of one's possessions and the issue of Jesus' concern shown for neglected, rejected, and oppressed persons. (One issue I didn't mention is the church's relationship to Judaism, to which Luke gives considerable attention.) It is assumed with considerable probability that Luke's audience consisted primarily of persons with more rather than less in terms of material possessions and of persons who were accepted and affirmed more than rejected and oppressed.

Since we will pursue here in greater depth Luke's second theme—concern for the marginal people—a few comments should be made in order to set the context on Luke's first concern of radical discipleship.

In comparison with Mark and Matthew, with whom Luke shares much in common, Luke always heightens or radicalizes the emphasis on discipleship and concern for material possessions. For some examples, consider the following. In Luke's account of the call of the first disciples (Peter, James, and John), Luke says: "they left everything and followed him" (Luke 5:11). Matthew and Mark do not use the term "everything." The "everything" may seem innocent at this point, but as one goes on in Luke into the story of the calling of Levi, Luke says: "he left everything . . . , and followed him" (Luke 5:28). The story in the other Gospels does not include the word "everything." When Jesus gives the challenge to his disciples to take up the cross to follow him, Luke writes: "take up [the] cross daily and follow me" (Luke 9:23). The other Gospels do not use the word "daily." I could go on with about twenty-five more examples, but I won't. The point is that Luke consistently follows this heightening and augments the heightening of radical discipleship with rearrangements that put otherwise disparate Jesus traditions together with Jesus traditions that are distinctively his own.

For example, consider Luke 12:13-34. In this text we find that unit of Jesus' teaching which begins: "Therefore I tell you, do not be anxious about your life, what you shall eat, nor about your body, what you shall put on" and ending with: "Instead, seek [God's] kingdom, and these things shall be yours as well" (Luke 12:22, 31). Of course, most of us, and the so-called "average" reader of the Bible as well, recognize these words as Sermon on the Mount material that we would probably first look for in Matthew 6:25-34.

Luke relocates this unit of Jesus' teaching and presents it with a different thrust by the new context in which he sets it. Luke prefaces this unit with two stories. The first story (Luke 12:13-15) concerns a dispute between two brothers over the inheritance that has been left to them, and the punch line comes in Jesus' response: "a [person's] life does not consist in the abundance of his possessions" (Luke 12: 15). The second story is the one that we have come to know as the parable of the rich fool. The punch line of that story, after the man builds his bigger barns and dies, is: "So is [one] who lays up treasure for [oneself], and is not rich toward God" (Luke 12:21). It can be observed that the rich fool is into barn building. Thus, the unit of Jesus' teaching with which we began has an added point when we read: "Consider the ravens . . . they have neither storehouse nor barn, and yet God feeds them" (Luke 12:24).

After the two stories and the unit of Jesus' teaching that ends with the appeal to seek God's kingdom, Luke has one more paragraph (Luke 12:33-34). This paragraph is virtually identical with Matthew 6:19-21 (material from an earlier point in the Sermon on the Mount than the "seek you first" passage). However, Luke distinctively introduces this final appeal to put one's treasure in heaven with these words: "Sell your possessions, and give alms . . . " (Luke 12:33).

Thus, Luke has packaged the Jesus tradition in 12:13-34 so that it sounds like this when you look at the whole: two brothers dispute and Jesus says: "one's life does not consist in the abundance of one's possessions." The rich fool dies and Jesus says: "one who lays up treasure for oneself is not rich toward God." Then there comes the appeal not to be anxious about one's life but to seek God's kingdom, climaxed with the statement: "Sell your possessions and give alms. For where your treasure is, there will your heart be also." My point is that Luke self-consciously and intentionally tells the story of Jesus to highlight the concern for radical discipleship and its impact on material possessions.

In the same way Luke shapes his Gospel to show that Jesus was a person who cared for persons who were marginalized. This care aspect of Luke is a broad theme that unites the whole of the Gospel and even Acts (Luke's second volume) where Luke is concerned with the inclusiveness and universality of the Gospel. Jesus' care for marginalized and oppressed persons as seen in the Gospel of Luke touches on seven groups of people: sinners, tax collectors, the poor, the physically maimed, women, Samaritans, and Gentiles. We will look at these seven categories in turn. In virtually every case the incidents and sayings used to illustrate these concerns occur only in Luke.

According to Luke, the first group of persons for whom Jesus showed special care were sinners. I think one of the most powerful stories in the Gospel of Luke occurs in 7:36-50, when Jesus goes to the home of Simon the Pharisee. Remember, there's no reason to think this man is particularly devious. He is a person who is genuinely seeking after

God and who hopes, like many others in Israel hoped, that someone might be the Messiah. He heard enough stories about Jesus to begin to think that perhaps Jesus was, in fact, the one who had been sent from God, and so he invited Jesus to his home. During dinner, you recall, a woman who was known to be a sinner came in and did not cease to kiss Jesus' feet during the dinner. Simon was disturbed that Jesus would allow this person to touch him. As a result Simon concluded that Jesus could not be from God; no one could come from God and allow a sinner to come that close. Jesus, on the other hand, noted that it was the sinner who loved him, and he declared that person saved, forgiven, made whole. Simon was forgotten.

The word "sinner" occurs four times in the Gospel of John, five times in the Gospel of Matthew, five times in the Gospel of Mark—and seventeen times in the Gospel of Luke (5:8, 30, 32; 6:32, 33, 34; 7:34, 37, 39; 13:2; 15:1, 2, 7, 10; 18:13; 19:7; 24:7). Without question, Luke is interested in the category "sinner." In Jesus' day a sinner was understood to be a person who did not subscribe to the Pharisaic interpretation of vigilant, rigorous adherence to the Law. It did not mean just persons who may have committed a particular immoral act or who might have been particularly devious in some way, but it meant the whole category of people who did not share the religious passion of the Pharisees.

Jesus befriended and spent time with sinners. This is noted again and again in Luke. Jesus picked up a nickname out of this context—a name that we have tended to accept as a friendly designation of Jesus in our piety, but which in Jesus' own time was a sneer. The nickname was: "friend of sinners" (Luke 7:34). That was one of the primary criticisms directed at Jesus by his critics. When Jesus is sneered at with the title "friend of sinners," Luke makes clear that it was God's intention and Jesus' mission to focus on sinners; that the Son of Man came to seek and to save sinners (5:32; 19:10). It is not surprising that when Peter is called he says, "I am a sinful man" (Luke 5:8); that the tax collector in the parable of the Pharisee and the tax collector says, "God, be merciful to me a sinner!" (18:13); and that when Jesus goes to the home of Zacchaeus, he is identified as a sinner (19:7). It is not surprising that only in the Gospel of Luke does Jesus turn to one of the criminals on the cross beside him and say, "today you will be with me in Paradise" (23:43). Thus, it is one of the climaxes of the Gospel of Luke when Jesus is surrounded by sinners and is again criticized for spending time with sinners that Jesus tells the three famous parables of the lost sheep, the lost coin, and the lost son (Luke 15). The point is that when a sinner repents, God has a party!

The second group of persons for whom Jesus showed special care (according to Luke) was tax collectors. Tax collectors in Jesus' day were persons who were especially disliked for two reasons. First, they cooperated with the Romans, who were seen as the occupying power in Palestine. Tax collectors were, to some extent, treasonous and traitorous to the very cause that eventually led the Jews in the first century to revolt against Rome. Second, the tax collectors were known for being dishonest and for fleecing people. The tax collectors are mentioned many times in Luke (3:12; 5:27, 29, 30; 7:29, 34; 15:1; 18:10, 11, 13; 19:2), always with sinners, save one time (3:12). They were a special group of sinners in the culture at that time. Jesus again is criticized for being with tax collectors. He is with them and calls one of them to be a disciple (Luke 5). He is with them as he preaches (Luke 7), and he is with them again when he tells the parables of the lost coin, the lost sheep, and the lost son (Luke 15).

John the Baptist preaches to tax collectors, anticipating the ministry of Jesus to tax collectors. We know what happens when Jesus calls Levi; he leaves everything and follows Jesus (Luke 5). When Jesus goes to Jericho—and it must be difficult for us to understand the actual social dynamic of Jesus arriving in Jericho, a very important city which must have had a lot of important people—he makes the decision to go to the home of Zacchaeus for a fellowship meal (Luke 19). Zacchaeus was one of the most despised, rejected persons in the city of Jericho, the last kind of person a decent, upstanding representative of God should be seen with. Jesus goes to the home of Zacchaeus, and we know what happens. The declaration is that that day salvation came to the house of Zacchaeus.

Only in Luke does Jesus tell the story of the two men who went into the temple to pray (Luke 18:9-14). The Pharisee, lifting his eyes to heaven, thanked God that he was not like the dishonest and extortionist tax collector, but that he was, in fact, a good man. He did tithe, he did pray, he did come to the temple. But he thanked God he wasn't like the tax collector. The tax collector, as you well know, did not lift his eyes to heaven, but cast his eyes downward and beat his breast and said, "God, be merciful to me a sinner." Jesus declared to his audience, primarily Pharisees, that it was the tax collector who had a right relationship with God.

The third group of persons for whom Jesus showed special

care (according to Luke) were the poor. The poor were marginalized in the Palestinian society of Jesus' day, generally
because the properly pious people were usually the ones
who had the positions of power, status, and economic access. The concern for the poor is replete throughout the
Gospel of Luke.

Probably the first case of dramatic concern for the poor is
Mary, the mother of Jesus, an unknown, unrecognized Galilean girl. When Luke records her praise to God, she thanks
God for having recognized the place of the poor and having
cast down the might of the rich (1:51-53). We go on in Luke
to Jesus' inaugural sermon (4:16-30) in Nazareth when he
quotes from Isaiah. Among the things that Jesus announces
for his own ministry in his inaugural sermon in Nazareth is
that he has been sent to preach to the poor. When John the
Baptist (in prison) begins to have doubts as to whether Jesus
really is the one that he had originally thought he was, he
sends a couple of his followers to interrogate Jesus (7:18-23)
and say: "Are you he who is to come, or shall we look for
another?" (7:19). Jesus doesn't say anything. He continues
to heal the sick, he continues to reach out to the people who
are around him, and then he turns to John's delegates and
says: "Go and tell John . . . [that] the poor have good news
preached to them" (Luke 7:22). That was Jesus' answer.
Later Jesus is invited again to the home of a Pharisee, a
religious leader, for dinner (14:1-24). There are many things
that happen at that dinner. Jesus communicates many mes-
sages in that context, but he does tell two stories while he
is sitting at the dinner in the home of this Pharisee with
many other fine persons, and they have identical punch

lines. In the first story Jesus says, "When you give a dinner or a banquet, do not invite your friends or your brothers or your kinsmen or rich neighbors, lest they also invite you in return, and you be repaid" (14:12). The punch line in these stories about people who are unresponsive to God's invitation, probably implying those in whose home Jesus was then eating, as given by Jesus is: "Here is who you should invite to dinner: the poor, the lame, the maimed and the blind (Luke 14:13, 21, paraphrased). Then there is the story of the rich man and Lazarus (16:19-31). Without elaborating that whole story, we know that the man who feasted sumptuously every day and never stopped to inquire about the beggar at his gate was not the one who ended up in the bosom of Abraham, even though he addressed him from hell as "Father Abraham." It was Lazarus who had the arms and protection of Abraham.

The explicit inclusion of the poor in the Gospel of Luke in the mission of Jesus is augmented and strengthened in many other passages about the poor, such as the Beatitudes: "Blessed are you poor" (not poor in spirit), (6:20); balanced by the woes, which are only in Luke. The Beatitudes and the woes are in immediate succession, the first woe being "Woe to you that are rich" (6:24). Blessed are the poor; woe to the rich. In addition consider: the passage in Luke 12 that we looked at earlier; the whole emphasis in Luke 16 is about using one's money to make friends for eternity; the story of the rich young ruler in Luke 18 (not unique to Luke); the widow's mite in Luke 21 (not unique to Luke); and the action of Zacchaeus, who, when he realized who Jesus was and turned to the salvation Jesus offered, gave half of his possessions to the poor (Luke 19).

The fourth group of persons for whom Jesus showed special care in Luke were the physically maimed. It was commonly believed that persons who were physically maimed were in some way under God's judgment. That is why when in the Gospel of John the disciples saw a man who was born blind (John 9), they asked Jesus what they probably thought was a very sophisticated theological question: Was it this man or his parents who sinned that he was born blind? They gave Jesus the options and misunderstood the whole idea.

Some of you know of the Qumran community that produced the Dead Sea Scrolls. They had very strict rules that had to do with physical perfection. The slightest physical disability, however temporary, would disqualify one from living in the community. One would have to leave until one could present oneself as physically acceptable. It was understood widely in Jesus' day that physical handicap, the maiming of the body, disqualified one from genuine care in any place in society.

Almost all of the texts about Jesus' care for these people have been mentioned because they often are grouped with others, but in Jesus' inaugural address (Luke 4), where he said he'd been sent to preach to the poor, he said he'd been sent also to bring healing to the lame and sight to the blind. When the representatives from John the Baptist arrive, the answer is "Tell John that the gospel is preached to the poor, that the lame walk, that the blind see and even the dead are raised" (Luke 7:22, paraphrased). In the home of the Pharisee previously mentioned (Luke 14), we have the double punch line when Jesus said, "Go out and invite the poor, the lame, the maimed and the blind" (Luke 14:13, 21, paraphrased). Jesus always cared for those persons.

The fifth group of persons for whom Jesus expressed special care in Luke were women. In the society of Jesus' day, women were greatly devalued. One of the most remarkable and difficult statements comes from Sirach, a pre-Pharisaic theological work written about 175 years before Jesus' time. Sirach 42:14 tells us: "Better is the wickedness of a man than a woman who does good. . . ." Understand the scale of values: the goodness of a man, the wickedness of a man, and then on down to the goodness of a woman.

With such a scale of values, no wonder the Jewish historian Josephus said that according to the law a woman is inferior in all things. The Jewish philosopher Philo and Josephus taught that a woman must never go outside of the home except in very specific circumstances with very specific procedures in view. In the earliest Rabbinic controversies about divorce, the leading party taught that a man could divorce his wife for any reason he pleased; women did not have the option of divorce.

Luke records more about Jesus' positive involvement with women than does the writer of any other Gospel. In the so-called infancy narratives (Luke 1–2), Elizabeth, Mary, and Anna are lifted up as important persons in God's announcement of salvation. Jesus uses a woman in the parable of the lost coin, and every finder in those parables is an image of God (Luke 15). Jesus allowed sinful and rejected women to approach him and touch him. Women who were considered unfit to touch anyone were given access to Jesus, such as the woman who kissed his feet (Luke 7) and the woman who had the twelve-year menstrual problem (Luke 8). Jesus had female disciples (8:1-3). Jesus teaches Mary in spite of the understanding that no Jewish male ever should teach a woman. Jesus commends and defends Mary when Martha, who has performed the traditional tasks, is upset (10:38-42). The women followers of Jesus were the first witnesses and the first proclaimers of the resurrection (Luke 24). As the story of Luke goes on into Acts, women continue to play a special role. Luke even notes that when the group gathered to wait for the coming of the Holy Spirit, the women were present (Acts 1:14).

The sixth group of persons for whom Jesus showed special care in Luke were the Samaritans. Most of us know that line from the Gospel of John that the Jews and Samaritans have no dealings with each other (4:9). The hostility between Jews and Samaritans by Jesus' time was enormous. There had been all kinds of theological and religious disputes as well as physical violence for over two hundred years. A group from Judea had gone up and burned the Samaritan temple. Samaritans regularly ambushed and killed Jewish travelers who came through Samaria.

In that context, think of the parable of the good Samaritan (Luke 10:29-37). That parable has been misunderstood in much of the history of the church. It's been moralized so that the point has been that the good Samaritan was nice—we should be nice, too; the good Samaritan did good deeds—we should do good deeds, too. That's why we have good Samaritan hospitals and good Samaritan nursing homes and good Samaritan awards and all these things. I think, rather, that the point of the story is related directly to the setting with the Jewish lawyer, who asked Jesus what one must do to have eternal life. The answer is to obey the command of God to love God and love your neighbor. Then Jesus tells the parable. The real point of the parable is that it was one of those despised, terrible, awful Samaritans who is lifted up as the one who obeyed God and God's command to love his neighbor, not someone in Israel. One of the people who was despised and rejected became a hero and example of faith.

Likewise, when Jesus heals the ten lepers, the one leper who comes back and praises God is the Samaritan. Jesus' reaction is: "Can't I find anybody in Israel who can praise God?" (Luke 17:18, paraphrased). It's consistent with the interpretation of the good Samaritan. Then, of course, in the book of Acts the gospel goes to Samaria (1:8; 8:4-25).

The seventh and last group of persons for whom Jesus shows special care in Luke are the Gentiles. From a Jewish point of view, the Gentiles were not particularly highly regarded. This can be illustrated with the story of Jesus and the Syrophoenician woman (Mark 7:24-30), to whom Jesus won't even talk at first, or in Paul's statement in Galatians 2:15 about "We ourselves, who are Jews by birth and not Gentile sinners. . . ." Deeply ingrained within the understanding of Judaism at that time was the conviction that they were close to God and Gentiles were far away.

Jesus reaches out to Gentiles, for which there are many references in the Gospel of Luke. In the infancy narrative Simeon holds the baby Jesus and says that he's a light of revelation to the Gentiles (2:32). John the Baptist preaches to soldiers and says, quoting Isaiah, " . . . all flesh shall see the salvation of God" (3:6). Jesus' ancestry in Luke isn't traced just to Abraham, but all the way back to Adam, so that Jesus can be the one for all people (3:23-38). In his inaugural sermon in Nazareth (4:16-30), after he quotes Isaiah, everybody is excited. They say, "This man is wonderful." Then Jesus tells two stories and they want to push him off the cliff. Why? Because in both stories the hero is a Gentile: the widow of Zarephath and Naaman the Syrian both are foreigners whom Jesus lifts up as exemplars of faith. Jesus pronounces woes on two Jewish Galilean cities— Chorazin and Bethsaida (10:13-15)—and says to those two cities that if the things that he had done in their cities had been done in Tyre and Sidon (foreign cities), they would have repented long ago. Jesus reaches out to Gentiles in every way in the Gospel of Luke. Then, as we know, it's the program of Acts that takes the gospel from Jerusalem to Judea, Samaria, and the whole world.

We see in Luke's distinctive, emphatic, clear presentation of Jesus' care the inclusiveness of the gospel for sinners, tax collectors, the poor, the physically maimed, women, Samaritans and Gentiles, and persons who in Jesus' time and place were rejected and oppressed. It should be noted that four times in Luke the phrase "Your faith has saved you" occurs. In every instance that word from Jesus comes to one of these persons. A sinner woman in Luke 7, an unclean woman in Luke 8, a Samaritan leper in Luke 17, and a blind beggar in Luke 18 all received the word "Your faith has saved you." This is why the story of the elder brother in Luke 15 is so important and so similar, in a way, to the story of Jonah. The elder brother represents the inability to understand the program and inclusiveness of Jesus' care. He can't come to the party. He cannot accept what Jesus demonstrates as a caring person.

If we are to be like Christ, we must let Luke's distinctive presentation of Jesus' care for marginal and oppressed people be for us instruction in caring. It also must model for us the inclusiveness of our commitment to the caring gospel.

The impact of Jesus' care for marginal and oppressed people should model for us our need to understand those for whom the church must care with integrity as part of its mission to bring all persons to the freeing, affirming, and maturing experience of gospel care.

Chapter 3

The Caring Community:

The Church as a Caring Community in Paul, Later New Testament Writers, and in Early Christianity

I realize that's a clumsy title. When you get past "The Caring Community" it's very cumbersome. Sometimes good titles are hard to come by. I am reminded of a student at Yale Divinity School a few years ago who was in a preaching class. One of the requirements was to turn in in sequence three sermons on a similar theme. This particular student submitted the first sermon, and the professor graded it and wrote comments on the written text saying that it was an excellent sermon, well developed, carefully argued, exegetically sound, gripping homiletically but, the professor said, "Your title is lousy." The title that the student had given his sermon was "The Ten Commandments." The professor said, "You need to get something that's really gripping and attractive; a title that, were it on the billboard in front of your church, would grab someone going by in a bus and make them want to get off the bus and come in and hear the sermon. Try to do better."

So the student handed in the second sermon. Again the

professor was impressed with the quality of the work but wrote on the paper, "Your title still is lousy." This time the student, in an effort to be responsive, titled the sermon "The Ten Commandments for Today." Again the professor wrote on the paper, "You should get a sermon title that would grab someone riding by on the bus so that they'd get off the bus and come in and hear your sermon."

It came time for the third sermon. This time the student turned it in, and the professor was overwhelmed. The title of the third sermon was "There's a Bomb on Your Bus!"

My primary interest here is to help us understand the early church as a caring community, both in its theological understanding of itself and its mission and also in its action in life. With such a perspective the early church's caring theology and lifestyle can be instructive for us as the people of God, both for ourselves and for our mission in the world.

There are two broad introductory concerns that I believe need to be addressed before we can approach and appropriately understand the early church as a caring community.

The first is to make certain that we avoid false idealism and misinformed romanticism in claiming the early church as a model. We must have integrity in assessing the early church as a caring group and institution. I think all of us have heard that desperate appeal, "Oh, if we could be like the early church."

All of us have come under the influence of Hegesippus whether we know it or not. Hegesippus was one of the earliest historians in the church. All of his writings were lost. But never fear, Eusebius, whom you have heard of, quoted Hegesippus on occasion. Hegesippus once said:

... until the time of Domitian [the Roman Emperor at the end of the first century] the church had remained a virgin, pure and uncorrupted . . . . But when the sacred band of the apostles had in various ways reached the end of their lives, and the generation of those privileged to listen with their own ears to the divine wisdom passed on, then godless error began to take shape . . . .[1]

Hegesippus was referring primarily to the rise of doctrinal controversy, but his image of a church pure and uncorrupted for the first two generations has contributed to the false perception of a romanticized, pure, loving early church.

In fact, the church was fraught with controversies from the very beginning. The earliest disputes in the church never were purely theological, but always were sociological realities that fused theological, social, cultural, and ethnic concerns into one reality.

The earliest dispute and controversy recorded for us is the one in Acts chapter 6. Too many of us have spent most of our lives either using it to prove something about deacons or to prove something not about deacons. But Acts 6 tells us that the Hellenists murmured against the Hebrews because their widows were neglected in the daily distribution. Hellenists were Greek-speaking Jews and the Hebrews were Aramaic-speaking Jews, two language groups in Jerusalem. Do we understand the conflict? The leaders were in conflict; the widows were neglected, and the issue was ethnic and cultural. The home-language folk were being favored in the daily distribution, and the Greek-speaking widows were not getting their share.

We find another early controversy in Galatians 2:11-14,

which relates a very famous incident in the church in Antioch. The Antioch church, which had become the exemplar of Jewish and Gentile inclusion, was having a meal together. The Jews and Gentiles were eating together, and Peter was there, Barnabas was there, and Paul was there (three of the dominant leaders of the church). A group came from Jerusalem who didn't appreciate eating with Gentiles. As soon as they entered the room, Peter got up and left. Then Paul said, "even Barnabas left." When we think that Barnabas was one who, in a sense, put his life on the line for the inclusion of the Gentiles, and recruited Paul, it really was a stunning controversy. Even the later church fathers (Augustine and Jerome) argued over whether Peter or Paul took the right approach this time. Of course Paul—and he's our only source for the story—was convinced he was right. But the conflict was a serious one. It was a cultural-theological conflict.

The problematic situation of Corinth has become a proverbial whipping post for problems in the early church. But notice especially what the basic issue was in Corinth: spiritual pride and the actual abuse of others through the neglect of edification, and especially the abuse at the Lord's Supper—where a couple of things happened that would be hard to duplicate in a Baptist church today. First, people got drunk at the Lord's Supper. Second, they deprived the poor of food. Perhaps we never have noticed that, but if we look again at 1 Corinthians 11:22, it has been called to our attention by the new sociological-exegetical movement in biblical studies that the Corinthians came together to eat, and those who had more and had more control were eating all the food and the poor were getting little or no food at all.

A later controversy, in the third century, is mentioned in the *Didascalia Apostolorum,* in which the care of the widows is discussed.

> Now we see and hear that there are widows in whom there is envy towards one another. For when thy fellow aged woman has been clothed, or has received somewhat from some one, thou oughtest, O widow, on seeing thy sister refreshed . . . to say: "Blessed be God who hath refreshed my fellow aged woman" and to praise God . . . . But now we hear that there are widows who do not behave according to the commandment, but care only for this, that they may stray and run about asking questions. Moreover, she who has received an alms of the Lord—being without sense in that she discloses the matter to those that ask her—has revealed the name of the giver; and the other hearing it murmurs and finds fault with the bishop who has dispensed . . . .[2]

I hope we understand that a widow was given a coat, and she told the other widows that she got a new coat and told them who gave it to her. The other widows were envious, and they went and complained to the bishop crying, "unfair distribution!"

The early church had a lot of problems. Many of their problems, although they had deep theological dimensions, were problems rooted in the very character of social life together among different kinds of people.

A second introductory concern has to do with a large, broad, and complex historical-sociological analysis of the nature of the early church and what made it a movement that survived and triumphed in antiquity. The early church did grow—from the 120 on the Day of Pentecost to a time within 400 years of dominating the social, political, and economic structures of the Roman Empire! This is a difficult question, on which there is no clear scholarly consensus. I want to present two viewpoints, however, and suggest a modest resolution.

Before we look at those viewpoints, it is important to get a sense of the temper of the times. What was the religious situation/mood of the Roman society into which the early church launched its proclamation of a caring gospel?

One of the classic attempts at such a definition comes from Gilbert Murray in his book *Five Stages of Greek Religion.* The first three stages cover the period before the time of the early church; the fifth stage covers a later time. It is the fourth stage that concerns the time of the Hellenistic-Roman period in which the church began and in which the church entered into its universal proclamation of the caring gospel. Gilbert Murray described the religious tenor of that time:

> It is hard to describe. It is a rise of asceticism, of mysticism, in a sense, of pessimism, a loss of self-confidence, of hope in this life and of faith in normal human effort; a despair of patient inquiry, a cry for infallible revelation; an indifference to the welfare of the state, a conversion of the soul to God. It is an atmosphere in which the aim of the good man is not so much to live justly, to help the society to which he belongs and enjoy the esteem of his fellow creatures; but rather, by means of a burning faith, by contempt for the world and its standards, by ecstasy, suffering and martyrdom, to be granted pardon for his unspeakable unworthiness, his immeasurable sins. There is an intensifying of certain spiritual emotions; an increase of sensitiveness, a failure of nerve.[3]

It is not too difficult to imagine the multifaceted ways in which the early church would speak to and relate to this "failure of nerve" in its setting.

Now we may consider briefly the two major contrasting viewpoints that attempt to explain in historical, social, and cultural terms why the early church survived opposition and persecution and expanded and triumphed.

The first typology of explanation I draw from Ramsay MacMullen, a historian of the Roman Empire, from his 1984 book *Christianizing the Roman Empire.* MacMullen argues, to oversimplify his case a little, that there were three major factors: first, the operation of a desire for blessings; second, a fear of physical pain; but most important of all, MacMullen argues, belief in miracles.[4] In other words, MacMullen argues that the single most important factor in the growth of the church was the Christian miracles, especially those that restored physical and mental health. He argues that people were attracted to the church because of its miracle-working power. There is support for this view in the debate between the pagan Celsus and the church father Origen[5] and in much of the earliest art of the Christian church that can be recovered archaeologically.[6]

The second typology, and the one that I prefer, is drawn from E. R. Dodds, another classicist, in his 1965 book *Pagan and Christian in an Age of Anxiety.* Dodds argues that there were four major factors in the success of the early church:[7] one, its very exclusiveness; two, its openness to all; three, the fact that it held out to the disinherited the promise of a better life in another world (in Dodds's words "Christianity wielded both a bigger stick and a juicier carrot");[8] but the most important reason, Dodds argues, was:

A Christian congregation was from the first a community in a much fuller sense than any corresponding group . . . . Love

of one's neighbor is not an exclusively Christian virtue, but
in our period, the Roman Empire, the Christians appear to
have practiced it much more effectively than any other group.
The church provided the essentials of social security . . . . But
even more important . . . than these material benefits was the
sense of belonging which the Christian community could
give.[9]

My modest resolution is to understand MacMullen and
Dodds as complementary. MacMullen has identified the
apologetic, external factor with which the church had to
grapple to succeed in its context, the competition in the
miraculous. Dodds has identified the internal, personal, and
social factors that made the church a movement and institution of attractiveness and retention.

If Dodds's analysis is correct, at least from one major
perspective, then it is of great importance and significance to
note with emphasis and clarity that the early church did
grow through caring and love. The care involved personal
affirmation and inclusion and involved material assistance
and social concern.

This perspective of care and love can be augmented by
another important insight from the perspective of cultural
anthropology as presented by Bruce Malina in his 1986 book
Christian Origins and Cultural Anthropology. In his book Malina
reflects on love and care as answers to problems in the early
church and writes:

The message is always that love, care, and concern can con-
quer all, that love can eliminate the strife and contention
which mar living on the planet. The real problem is that love
involves both the free crossing of purity boundaries and the
elimination of many of the purity lines that define and de-

limit the sets of related rights and obligations that constitute meaningful society. Love has something chaotic about it in that to some extent it necessarily eliminates the lines that constitute order and meaning.[10]

With the importance of love and care in mind for understanding a crucial aspect of the early church and a sense of the ways in which love and care can be "chaotic," let us turn, then, to a selective analysis of the early church as a caring community as seen in Paul and some later writers.

Paul, of course, is one of the giants of the early church—so much a giant that many people have difficulty understanding Paul as a person like us. Paul often has been put in what I would judge to be a misconstrued framework, so that Paul is understood primarily as a theologian, even as a systematic theologian. Coupled with Paul's powerful role in the Reformation, it often has been difficult for people in the church to think of Paul as having anything practical to say. Paul is the darling of phrases like "justification by faith." Paul is the darling of persons who have used him for hundreds of years in the church as a set of texts to elaborate a systematic, carefully structured theology.

There was a time when I taught at Gordon-Conwell Seminary that we allowed students to take any New Testament course or set of courses they wished to meet the requirements. After three years of that we did a statistical study and discovered that all the students (more or less) who came from a Presbyterian or Reformed background took the introduction to Paul and all the students who came from Pentecostal, Holiness, Arminian, and Methodist backgrounds took the introduction to Jesus. This illustrated how Paul was perceived. He was the darling of a particular theological construct that did not deal with some of the moral imperatives that were easily understood to have surrounded Jesus.

What I want to suggest is that Paul, rightly understood, is a major theologian *and* an advocate of a caring style for the church. I will look at six representative passages in Paul's writings to illustrate that. The first is 1 Corinthians 12, the famous text about the body and the body image. Here Paul makes the point that there is one Body in Christ. All those who believe are baptized into one Body whether they are Jew or Greek, slave or free, male or female. They are all part of this one Body, and every person is a member of that Body, and every person in that Body has a function. The function is to assist everyone else in the Body to grow, mature, develop, and reach what God intends for a person. Paul concludes that discussion by saying:

> But God has so composed the body . . . that there may be no discord in the body, but that the members may have the same care for one another. If one member suffers, all suffer together; if one member is honored, all rejoice together (12:24-26).

The second text is in Philippians 2:1-4, which reads in part:

> . . . by being of the same mind, having the same love, being in full accord and of one mind. Do nothing from selfishness or conceit, but in humility count others better than yourselves. Let each of you look not only to [one's] own interests, but also to the interests of others (2:2-4).

That is illustrated in various ways in Philippians. One of the most remarkable passages in Philippians occurs in 1:15-18, where Paul, in prison, comments on the fact that there are other missionary preachers who now are having their glory days. Paul is in prison, and they have a chance to get the spotlight. Out of envy and jealousy these persons are opportunistic in preaching the gospel. In spite of all that, Paul says, "I rejoice that the gospel is preached" (1:18, paraphrased). Remarkable. He took his own words to heart to look not only to his own interests but also the interests of others.

Consider Timothy, described later in 2:19-24. Paul says, "I have no one like him, who will be genuinely anxious for your welfare" (2:20). Then there comes what must be a quotation of a saying of the day: "They all look after their own interests, not those of Jesus Christ" (2:21). It generally must have been understood that what people did was look after their own interests. What singled Timothy out was that he genuinely was caring for the welfare of the Philippians.

Consider Epaphroditus (2:25-30), about whom Paul says " . . . he nearly died for the work of Christ, risking his life to complete your [Philippian] service to me" (2:30). Epaphroditus was so much a servant of the Philippian church that he nearly died in carrying out their mission.

It is in these contexts that we should see the famous passage in Philippians 2:5-11 about Christ: "Have this mind among yourselves, which is yours in Christ Jesus . . . " (2:5). Like Paul, like Timothy, and like Epaphroditus, Christ also considered the interests of others and took upon himself the form of a servant.

The third passage in Paul I want to note is Romans chapters 12 and 13. Here again is the Body image and the affirmation that every member has a gift and a function, very

THE CARING GOD

similar to 1 Corinthians 12. There also is a statement in Romans 12 that one ought not to think of oneself more highly than one should (very similar to the passage in Philippians 2). Then in Romans 12:9 Paul says, "Let love be genuine." This is followed by 19 participles, two infinitives, and three imperatives (in Greek) all of which function as elaborations of the statement: "Let love be genuine." They are explanatory subordinate injunctions, so that each of the following twenty-four statements in Romans 12:9-21 is an explanation of what genuine love is. I would make the recommendation for some caring exercise to do a Bible study with others on what is genuine love, and let those twenty-four statements define what genuine love is. Then in Romans 13, as a climax to this discussion, Paul says, "Love does no wrong to a neighbor; therefore love is the fulfilling of the law" (13:10).

The fourth passage in Paul that I want to note is 1 Corinthians chapters 8–10. The issue here is eating meat that has been offered to idols and is served especially in pagan temples. Some of the believers in the Corinthian church say it's perfectly all right to go into a temple and eat meat that has been sacrificed to an idol because we know that idols don't exist. There is only one God. Paul says, "You're right. You're theologically pure and right. But your caring is wrong." "Therefore," Paul says in 8:13, "if food is a cause of my brother's [or sister's] falling, I will never eat meat, lest I cause [one of them] to fall." Paul climaxes that whole long, somewhat contorted and tortuous discussion that goes all the way to the end of chapter 10 with these words: " . . . do all to the glory of God. Give no offense to Jews or to Greeks or to the church of God, just as I try to please all . . . in everything

I do, not seeking my own advantage . . . " (10:31-33). Paul's agenda—to give no offense to anybody—may produce conflict and ambiguity, but what I think should be noted is that it is other-directed and inclusive of the whole society. Paul is concerned not only for the church but also for the Jews and the Greeks, the components of the society in which he lived.

The fifth text I want to note is Galatians chapters 5 and 6. Listen to these words from Galatians, the text that has been celebrated as much as any as the text about justification by faith: "For in Christ Jesus neither circumcision nor uncircumcision is of any avail, but **faith working through love**" (5:6, emphasis mine); "For you were called to freedom . . . ; only do not use your freedom as an opportunity for the flesh, **but through love be servants of one another**" (5:13, emphasis mine); " . . . if [anyone] is overtaken in any trespass, you who are spiritual should restore [that one] in a spirit of gentleness. Look to yourself, lest you too be tempted. **Bear one another's burdens,** and so fulfil the law of Christ" (6:1-2, emphasis mine); and the closing injunction of Galatians: "**And let us not grow weary in well-doing,** for in due season we shall reap, if we do not lose heart. So then, as we have opportunity, **let us do good to all** . . . , and especially to those who are of the household of faith" (6:9-10, emphasis mine). Galatians presents Paul as a caring pastoral theologian as much as any other image it gives us of Paul.

The last passage from Paul I would like to note is 2 Corinthians chapters 8 and 9. These two chapters focus on the offering Paul was collecting for the poor in Jerusalem, which he was collecting in Asia Minor (present-day Turkey), Macedonia (northern Greece), and Achaia (southern Greece). This offering has at least three deep ecclesial implications for understanding the church as a caring community. The first is the recognition of interchurch cooperation and responsibility. The New Testament says very little explicitly about how churches related to one another, but this offering is one of the clearest by implication. They worked together to collect the offering; they were bound together by the offering, and the offering was designated for another church. Second, the church in Jerusalem to which the offering was to go was a church beyond the personal involvement and experience of most of the churches in which the offering was collected. The churches in Asia Minor, Macedonia, and Achaia, for the most part, would have been made up of Gentile persons who probably never had been to Jerusalem, didn't understand what it meant to be a poor person in Jerusalem, and didn't understand what it meant to be a Jewish person in Jerusalem. Third is the recognition of the compatibility between the spiritual and the material. Paul argues in Romans that if the Gentile churches got their spiritual blessings out of Judaism, then it only logically followed that they should give their material blessings back to Jerusalem (15:27). There is absolutely no embarrassment or sense of tension between the interplay of the spiritual blessing and the material response. It is fascinating that in this context of 2 Corinthians chapters 8 and 9 there occurs what may be the earliest statement by any author of the church of the pre-existence of Christ: "Christ . . . though he was rich . . . he became poor" (8:9). Scholars debate whether that is a reference to the pre-existence of Christ, but I think it most probably is. What is significant is that what then becomes a debate of intense theological activity for the next 300 and more years in the church—having to do with the ontological nature of Christ—makes its first appearance as a practical argument to give money to the poor in Jerusalem: Christ, though he was rich, became poor; therefore, you folk in Achaia ought to give money to the poor in Jerusalem!

Although no summary can capture the richness, depth, and breadth of Paul's perspectives, an attempt to get the basic motif may be helpful for us. There are two major theological themes that come through these texts. The first is the example of Christ's incarnation, the second is the understanding that the church is one Body with many members. The Christian faith may be personal, but it is never private. The three major actions of caring in Paul are humility (considering others better than oneself), love (the genuine practicality of reaching out as a fulfillment of God's law), and the bearing of one another's burdens (seeking to identify with others in their sorrow or joy and actually contributing out of one's resources to meet the needs of others).

There are many passages other than Paul's that speak to the question of the early church as a caring community. In Hebrews there are some powerful texts about the church needing to meet together in order to provoke one another to love and good works. The church must meet together to do that (10:24-25; 6:10; 10:32-34). The passage in James, of course, is simply stunning about what it means to have genuine faith (2:15-16).

For years First John has been for me the most pointed of all the texts in the New Testament when it comes to the matter of caring. The writer of First John understands Jesus' self-sacrifice as the theological basis for genuine, tangible care for others: "By this we know love, that [Jesus] laid down his life for us; and we ought to lay down our lives for the [brothers and sisters]" (3:16). But this laying down of one's life is not literal martyrdom, for in the very next sentence 1 John 3:17-18 tells us what it means to lay down our lives following the example of Jesus:

> But if any one has the world's goods and sees his [sister or] brother in need, yet closes [one's] heart against [such a one], how does God's love abide in [that one]? Little children, let us not love in word or speech but in deed and in truth.

The whole theological rationale for loving one another is then spelled out (1 John 4): God initiated love; thus, love is a characteristic of the caring early church because God loved. That's repeated over and over again, especially in a text often quoted: "We love [him], because he first loved us" (4:19), but the "him" is not in the original text. In the context it is saying that we love one another because God first loved us. This comes to the climax in 4:20, which I find today still the most haunting, pressing, challenging, theological profundity about caring in the New Testament:

> If any one says, "I love God," and hates [a] brother [or sister], [that one] is a liar; for [the one] who does not love brother [or sister], whom [one] has seen, cannot love God whom [one] has not seen.

Early Christians, beyond the New Testament, also were a caring community. We need to recall those words of E. R. Dodds that the early church practiced community more effectively than any other group in the Roman Empire and that that was probably the primary reason for its survival and growth. The classicist Glanville Downey once wrote:

Not all Christians today realize the extent to which the early church was responsible for the innovation of welfare and organized charity . . . . Pagan society normally made no such provision for the needy. There was philanthropic impulse and philanthropic practice, to be sure, in the pre-Christian Graeco-Roman world. But such philanthropy was conceived and carried out entirely on an individual basis and to a very strictly limited extent.[11]

Of all the texts that one could look at I think pride of place would go to Tertullian's *Apology,* Chapter 39. Tertullian was a North African Carthaginian layperson who wrote many books. He didn't like women in ministry and had a lot of other ideas that were very interesting. He wrote the first book on baptism in the history of the church. He wrote *Apology* about A.D. 200 to defend the legitimacy of the Christian church. In Chapter 39 he described what it was like for the church to meet together. It's a long description that I've cut down here to just the "bare bones" of what he says:

We form one body because of our religious convictions, and because of the divine origin of our way of life in the bond of common hope. We come together for a meeting and a congregation, in order to besiege God with prayers, like an army in battle formation. Such violence is pleasing to God. We assemble for the consideration of the Holy Scriptures, [to see] if the circumstances of the present times demand that we look ahead or reflect. At the same occasion, there are words of encouragement, of correction, of holy censure. Certain approved elders preside, men who have obtained this honor not by money, but by the evidence of good character. For, nothing that pertains to God is to be had for money.

Even if there is some kind of treasury, it is not accumulated from a high initiation fee as if the religion were something bought and paid for. Each man deposits a small amount on a certain day of the month or whenever he wishes, and only on the condition that he is willing and able to do so. No one is forced; each makes his contribution voluntarily. These are, so to speak, the deposits of piety. The money therefrom is not spent for banquets or drinking parties or good-for-nothing eating houses, but for the support and burial of the poor, for children who are without parents and means of subsistence, for aged men who are confined to the house, for ship-wrecked sailors, and for any in the mines, on islands or in prisons. The practice of such a special love brands us in the eyes of some and they say "See how they love one another"; (for they hate one another) and "see how ready they are to die for each other." (They themselves would be more ready to kill each other.)

So, we who are united in mind and soul have no hesitation about sharing what we have. Every thing is common among us—except our wives. In this matter—which is the only mat-ter in which the rest of men practice partnership—we dis-solve partnership.

Why wonder, then, if such dear friends take pride in their meals together? Our meal together by its very name indicates its purpose. It's called by a name which to the Greeks means "love," agape. Whatever it costs, it is gain to incur expense in the name of piety, since by this refreshment we comfort the needy, not as among you, parasites contend for the glory of reducing their liberty to slavery for the price of filling their belly amidst insults, but as, before God, greater consideration is given to those of lower station. No one sits down to the table without first partaking of a prayer. They eat as much as those who are hungry take; they drink as much as temper-ate people need. After this, the hands are washed and the lamps are lit, and each one, according to his ability to do so, reads the Holy Scripture or is invited into the center to sing a hymn to God. This is the test of how much he has drunk.

Similarly, prayer puts an end to the meal. Such is the gathering of Christians.[12]

Tertullian is sterling evidence that the early church understood itself to be, above all, a caring community. Without doubt the early church *was* a caring community. Whatever its problems and failures, the early church did grow through caring. The legacy of the early church for Christians today in quest of our integrity is its theological understanding of itself, its mission, and its actualization of that understanding in life and action as a genuinely caring community.

Notes

Chapter 1

[1] E. Wiesel, *Night,* trans. S. Rodway (New York: Farrar, Strauss & Giroux, Inc. 1960; reprinted New York: Bantam Books Inc., 1982), p. 32 (Bantam).

[2] S. C. Guthrie, Jr., *Christian Doctrine: Teachings of the Christian Church* (Atlanta: John Knox Press, 1968), pp. 242–243.

[3] F. Holmgren, *The God Who Cares: A Christian Looks at Judaism* (Atlanta: John Knox Press, 1979).

[4] C. Klein, *Anti-Judaism in Christian Theology,* trans. E. Quinn (Philadelphia: Fortress Press, 1978).

[5] See the sophisticated and detailed analysis provided by E. P. Sanders, *Paul and Palestinian Judaism: A Comparison of Patterns of Religion* (Philadelphia: Fortress Press, 1977), especially pp. 1–24; 419–428; 543–556.

[6] S. Mark Heim, "Christian Faith in a Pluralistic World," in *Is Christ the Only Way?* (Valley Forge: Judson Press, 1985), p. 145.

[7] E.g., Exodus 22:22; Deuteronomy 10:18; 15:4-11; Psalms 68:5, 10; 82:3; 140:12; 145:9; Isaiah 1:17.

Chapter 2

[1] J. Pelikan, *Jesus Through the Centuries: His Place in the History of Culture* (New Haven and London: Yale University Press, 1985).

[2] *Ibid,* p. ix.

Chapter 3

[1] Eusebius, "Ecclesiastical History 3.32" *Eusebius, The History of the Church,* trans. G. A. Williamson (Harmondsworth/New York: Penguin Books, 1965), p. 143.

[2] *Didascalia Apostolorum* 3.10 (R. H. Connolly), *Didascalia Apostolorum: The Syriac Version Translated and Accompanied by the Verona Latin Fragments, with an Introduction and Notes* (Oxford: Clarendon, 1929), section XV, pp. 142–143.

[3] G. Murray, *Five Stages of Greek Religion,* 3d ed. (Boston: Beacon Press, 1951; reprinted Garden City: Doubleday and Co. Inc, n.d.), p. 119 (Doubleday).

[4] R. MacMullen, *Christianizing the Roman Empire (A.D. 100–400)* (New Haven and London: Yale University Press, 1984), p. 108.

[5] H. Chadwick, *Origen: Contra Celsum; Translated with an Introduction & Notes* (Cambridge: University Press, 1953).

[6] G. F. Snyder, *Ante Pacem: Archaeological Evidence of Church Life Before Constantine* (Macon: Mercer University Press, 1985), especially pp. 165–166.

[7] E. R. Dodds, *Pagan and Christian in an Age of Anxiety: Some Aspects of Religious Experience from Marcus Aurelius to Constantine* (The Wiles Lectures, 1963; Cambridge: University Press, 1965), pp. 133–138.

[8] *Ibid.,* p. 135.

[9] *Ibid.,* pp. 136–137.

[10] B. J. Malina, *Christian Origins and Cultural Anthropology: Practical Models for Biblical Interpretation* (Atlanta: John Knox Press, 1986), p. 58.

[11] G. Downey, "Who Is My Neighbor? The Greek and Roman Answer," *Anglican Theological Review 47,* 1965, p. 3.

[12] Tertullian, *Apology* 39 (trans. R. Arbesmann, E. J. Daly and E. A. Quain), *Tertullian, Apologetical Works and Minucius Felix, Octavius; Fathers of the Church* 10 (New York: Fathers of the Church, 1950), pp. 98–102 (selections).